CHRIS HOY BIOGRAPHY BOOK

The Untold Story of the Britain's Most Decorated Olympian

By Greg Davis

Copyright © 2024 by Greg Davis

All rights reserved. No part of this publication may be reproduced, distributed, or transmitted in any form or by any means, including photocopying, recording, or other electronic or mechanical methods, without the prior written permission of the publisher, except in the case of brief quotations embodied in critical reviews and certain other noncommercial uses permitted by copyright law

Table of Contents

Introduction **4**

Chapter 1 ....**8**

Chris Hoy: His Early Years.....................**8**

Chapter 2 ....**16**

Chris Hoy's Professional Journey: Cycling Begins **16**

Chapter 3 ....**25**

Chris Hoy's Development: Rise to Fame in Track Cycling **25**

Chapter 4 ....**32**

Olympic Triumphs for Hoy: London (2012), Beijing (2008), and Athens (2004) **32**

Chapter 5 ....**40**

The World Championship Accomplishments and Retirement of Professional Cyclist Sir Chris Hoy..........**40**

Chapter 6 ....**47**

3 | P a g e

After-Cycling Career and Chris Hoy's Non-Sport Life 47

Introduction

A retired British track cyclist, Sir Chris Hoy is considered by many to be among the best Olympic cyclists of all time. Born in Edinburgh, Scotland, on March 23, 1976, Hoy's incredible career lasted more than 20 years, making him the most successful Olympic athlete in Great Britain until Jason Kenny broke his record in 2021. Hoy got his start in riding when he was seven years old and began competing in BMX races. In a short period of time, he demonstrated promise by winning the Scottish BMX championship and placing second in Britain and ninth globally. Hoy made the switch to track cycling as he got older, which would eventually lead to his Olympic success.

Hoy took home a silver medal in the team sprint at the UCI Track Cycling World Championships in 1999, his first significant international medal. With this accomplishment, he launched a brilliant career that would see him rule the track cycling world for many years to come. Hoy made his Olympic debut in 2000, competing for the British team sprint squad and winning a silver medal. His ambition was stoked by this early success, and he eagerly returned to the Olympics in Athens four years later. A pivotal moment in Hoy's career occurred during the 2004 Summer Olympics in Athens. His first Olympic gold medal came in the 1km time trial, where he also set an Olympic record. With this triumph, Hoy not only became a formidable force in international cycling but also signaled the start of a golden age for British cycling.

However, Hoy's reputation as a cycling legend was solidified during the 2008 Beijing Olympics. In a single Games, he won three gold medals in the keirin, team sprint, and individual sprint events, demonstrating incredible skill and dominance. With his three gold medal haul, he became the first British Olympian to win three gold medals at an Olympic Games since swimmer Henry Taylor in 1914. Hoy's triumph in Beijing greatly boosted Team GB's overall performance, inspiring a new generation of British cyclists and raising awareness of the sport in the UK. The 2009 New Year Honours list named him Sir Chris Hoy in recognition of his accomplishments.

The 2012 London Games marked the end of Hoy's Olympic career. Hoy won two more gold medals while competing domestically, taking first place in the keirin and team sprint competitions. These wins made him the most successful British Olympian at the time, bringing his total Olympic medal count to seven (six gold and one silver). Hoy's career includes two gold medals from the Commonwealth Games and eleven world championship titles in addition to his Olympic success. He has continuously performed at the top level and broken multiple world records in a variety of track cycling events, such as the sprint, team sprint, keirin, and time trial.

Hoy's influence on cycling in Britain goes well beyond his own accomplishments. He was an important part of British Cycling's elite performance program and helped the team become well-known worldwide. Together with his teammates Bradley Wiggins and Victoria Pendleton, he inspired a new generation of cyclists and helped turn Britain into a cycling powerhouse. Hoy has had a significant impact off the track by advocating for cycling and sports in general. He has been a part of several campaigns to promote cycling at all levels, from amateur to professional racing. A reminder of his legacy and contribution to the sport is the Sir Chris Hoy Velodrome in Glasgow, which was constructed for the 2014 Commonwealth Games.

After retiring from competitive cycling in 2013, Hoy has continued to be involved in sports. In addition to being an author of multiple books, including an autobiography and a number of children's books, he has worked as a commentator and analyst for major cycling events and has participated in a number of charitable activities.

It is still clear that Sir Chris Hoy and his peers laid the groundwork for British cycling's success on the global scene. His impact on track cycling and Olympic sport, both domestically and internationally, guarantees that his name will go down as one of the greatest in history.

Chapter 1
Chris Hoy: His Early Years

British race car driver and cyclist Chris Hoy was born in Edinburgh, Scotland, on March 23, 1976. One of the most accomplished athletes in Britain, he has won six gold medals at the Olympics. At what is now the Royal Infirmary of Edinburgh, the Simpson Memorial Maternity Pavilion, he was born. The family Chris was born into had a strong Scottish heritage, with roots ingrained in the history and culture of the nation. He is Christopher Andrew Hoy in full. He was born and raised in the Scottish capital, where he developed an early passion for sports and exercise. David Hoy, his father, was a businessman, and Carol Hoy, his mother, was a nurse. In their pursuits, Chris and his younger sister Carrie received encouragement from both parents. Although his family wasn't very active in cycling at first, Chris became interested in a variety of sports, with BMX (Bicycle Motocross) being the first to capture his interest.

David and Carol Hoy, his parents, played a significant role in influencing his formative years and creating the atmosphere that would eventually result in one of Britain's most prosperous Olympians. Carol was a nurse at the Royal Infirmary of Edinburgh, and David Hoy was for the Registers of Scotland as a surveyor. The couple gave Chris and his sister Carrie a secure and nurturing home environment. Originally from the Scottish Borders, Chris's paternal grandfather, Andy Hoy, was a farmer. Chris's passion for the outdoors and exercise would later be influenced by this rural connection. Instilling a sense of discipline and patriotism in the family, Chris's mother's side grandfather had served in the Royal Air Force during World War II.

Being raised in Edinburgh's Murrayfield neighborhood, Chris had access to a wide range of outdoor and sports activities. The Murrayfield Ice Rink and Murrayfield Stadium, the site of Scottish rugby matches, were both close to the family's residence. Chris was exposed to a culture of athleticism and competition at a young age thanks to these local sporting events. When Chris was just six years old, he got his first bicycle as a Christmas gift, which marked the beginning of his cycling adventures. Chris adapted to the small BMX bike right away. Riding around the neighborhood for hours on end helped him hone his coordination and balance, which would later be useful in his cycling career.

Hoy began cycling when he was seven years old, and until 1991, he competed in BMX racing. He then briefly tried mountain biking. Moreover, he competed for Scotland in junior rowing. He began riding track bikes in 1992, and in 1994 he won his first medal at the British Championship, a silver in the junior sprint division.

Even after students graduate from school, teachers can influence them in a lasting way by making subjects and activities interesting. Chris went to George Watson's College in Edinburgh, which influenced other facets of his life in addition to his career. He had a great time there and still keeps up with the friends he made there. Aside from academics, the school encouraged students to follow their passions, which for Chris meant mostly sports. Math in particular piqued his interest, and he relished the challenge of problem-solving. A variety of sports were played by Chris during his elementary school years. He continued to ride a bike for fun, played rugby, and attempted gymnastics. By allowing him to experiment with different sports, the school's extensive physical education curriculum helped him build a diverse range of physical abilities.

He had a number of favorite teachers in school, especially those who were able to relate to the students and were enthusiastic about their subjects. His decision to pursue history was primarily impacted by an engaging instructor who brought the subject to life. Football, rugby, athletics, and rowing were among Chris's many extracurricular activities. He began cycling at an early age, competing in BMX from the age of seven to fourteen before progressing to road, mountain, and track cycling. Trying a range of sports and activities allowed Chris to experiment with different interests before deciding on one, which he felt was important. You're more likely to discover what really works for you if you have more experiences.

In 1997, Hoy's career took a significant turn when the British Cycling Federation introduced its World Class Performance Plan, which gave him financial assistance while he finished his education. He earned a silver medal in the team sprint at the 1999 Senior World Championship, the same year he received his degree in sports science from the University of Edinburgh. It was a rare display of emotion from the usually reticent Scot, whose discipline and control are the foundation of his professional style. Years of perseverance and hard work, however, were reflected in that moment on the Velodrome podium. Chris Hoy, the son of David and Carol Hoy, grew up in Edinburgh's Murrayfield neighborhood. Before moving to the University of Edinburgh, where he graduated in 1999 with a Bachelor of Science (Hons.) in Applied Sports Science, he studied mathematics and physics for two years at the University of St Andrews after attending George Watson's College.

Chris loved playing a lot of different sports as a kid, but it was a fortuitous experience with cycling as a competitive sport that would shape his future. Chris and his father traveled to Edinburgh for the Commonwealth Games when Chris was seven years old. This was 1984, and his hometown was hosting the Games. Chris first got to see track cycling when they went to the velodrome. He was captivated by the fierce competition, the speed, and the shiny bikes. Motivated by his observations, Chris started to take cycling more seriously. One of Scotland's oldest cycling clubs, Dunedin Cycling Club, is the one he joined. It was here that he started learning the basics of competitive cycling, such as track and road racing techniques.

Hoy demonstrated his athletic ability at a young age. In his teenage years, he was a standout rugby player at George Watson's College. At 14, he competed in BMX for both Scotland and Great Britain, winning the Scottish title and finishing second in the UK. In the British Championship coxless pairs, he won a silver medal for Scotland. He also experimented with mountain biking and rowing. During his early and adolescent years, Chris's family was instrumental in helping him pursue his cycling goals. While supporting his passion, his parents also made sure he led a balanced life. David, Chris's father, served as both his first manager and coach for cycling. He would transport Chris to sporting events throughout Scotland and, eventually, the United Kingdom. The foundation of Chris's support network would be this father-son relationship, which was developed via innumerable training and travel hours. Carrie, Chris's sister, was also a big part of his early life. Even though she was three years younger than him, she was one of his strongest supporters and frequently went to Chris's races with the family. The siblings were very close, and Carrie helped keep things normal and supported Chris's emotionally taxing cycling schedule. The Dunedin Cycling Club's coaches served as mentors to Chris outside of his family.

Influenced by the BMX bike that was shown in the 1982 movie E.T. When Hoy was six years old, he developed a passion for riding a bicycle. During his time racing BMX from the ages of 7 to 14, he placed second in Britain, fifth in Europe, and ninth globally. He participated in both European and American competitions, sponsored by Slazenger and Kwik-Fit. Scots sprinter Eddie Alexander's bronze medal at the 1986 Commonwealth Games in Edinburgh sparked his interest in track cycling. Aside from cycling, Hoy competed for the Scotland Junior Rowing Team and finished second in the coxless pairs at the 1993 National Rowing Championships with Grant Florence. He was also a rugby player for his school. With the Dunedin club and then the City of Edinburgh Racing Squad, the best cycling team in the UK at the time, Hoy turned his entire focus to track cycling in 1992. After joining the British national team four years later, he had a slow start but, with perseverance, he soon overtook his teammates to become the team's top sprinter in two years.

As Chris grew through his adolescence, his list of accomplishments on the bike expanded quickly. By the age of 14, he was starting to establish himself on the national scene and competing in competitions all over Scotland. When Chris was sixteen years old, he won his first British Championship title in the Junior Sprint division in 1992. He became one of the most promising young cyclists in the nation with this victory, which was a major turning point. Chris went to the Junior World Championships in Perth, Australia, the following year, representing Great Britain. Despite the fact that he did not receive a medal, the experience of competing internationally was priceless. He got to know the top young cyclists in the world and got a preview of the kind of competition he would encounter later on. There were difficulties in Hoy's early cycling career. The infrastructure and resources that were available in other nations with more established cycling traditions, like France or Italy, were absent from track cycling in the UK, particularly in Scotland. Hoy was able to overcome these challenges, though, thanks to his perseverance and work ethic. He put in endless training and started to establish himself in the British cycling community. Coach Ray Harris was a pivotal figure in Hoy's early career; he saw his potential and assisted him in honing the technical skills necessary for track cycling success.

Chapter 2
Chris Hoy's Professional Journey: Cycling Begins

When he was younger, Hoy was fascinated by movement and speed, which he initially investigated through BMX racing rather than track cycling. The 1980s saw a rise in BMX's popularity, especially after movies like E.T. BMX bikes were featured prominently in the Extra-Terrestrial (1982). At six years old, Hoy requested a BMX bike after being influenced by the movie's BMX scenes. Following his parents' approval, he started getting really involved in the BMX scene.

After joining a BMX club, Hoy started participating in regional and national events. By the time he was fourteen, he was one of the best BMX riders in Europe and second in Britain. His time spent riding BMX was crucial to his growth as an athlete because it sharpened his control, balance, and competitive spirit, all of which he would later use to his advantage on the track. Even though he was successful in BMX at an early age, Hoy's teenage interests in sports grew beyond cycling. He played a variety of sports at George Watson's College, one of Edinburgh's top independent schools. Particularly in rowing, he was exceptionally good and even became a Scottish Junior Champion. For some time, rowing became his main activity, and Hoy thought about making it his career. Hoy experimented with the sports of rugby and athletics in addition to rowing. Hoy's cycling career reached a turning point in his mid-teens. In 1991, he made the decision to transition from BMX to track cycling at the age of 15. BMX was still a relatively new and unestablished sport at the time, so the desire to concentrate on a more structured and professional cycling path was one of the factors that drove this transition.

Hoy joined a reputable cycling club that developed young riders, the City of Edinburgh Racing Club. He first came into contact with organized coaching and track cycling training through this club. He adapted quickly to the discipline and discovered that his experience with BMX gave him a competitive advantage when it came to handling and sprinting on the track.

Hoy made waves in the Scottish and British cycling scenes after it became clear that he had a talent for track cycling. He began riding in track events in 1992 when he was sixteen years old and joined Dunedin CC, his first cycling club. The British national junior team invited him to join them after national selectors noticed his innate talent and commitment to training. After making quick progress, the young cyclist made his Great Britain debut in 1996. In the same year, he participated in the Junior World Championships and won his first world title with the junior sprint team. The foundation for Hoy's incredible senior career was laid by this early success, which was a sign of greatness to come. From the beginning, Hoy showed his commitment to his new sport. He started riding junior track under the tutelage of seasoned coaches at the City of Edinburgh Racing Club and quickly achieved success. In the British track cycling scene, Hoy had already established himself by the age of 18. He climbed through the ranks fast because he was faster, stronger, and more determined than many of his peers. During his transition into senior competition, Hoy kept honing his craft. His specialty was sprinting, specifically the team sprint, the keirin, and the kilo (1000-meter time trial). His strong physique and lightning-fast speed made these disciplines ideal for him, and his strength and strategic thinking enabled him to win races.

Hoy's efforts were rewarded, and he kept winning at national tournaments. Due to his achievements, he was accepted into the British Cycling Academy, a distinguished training program created to identify and develop the nation's best young athletes. The academy helped Hoy improve as a cyclist by giving him access to top-notch coaching, facilities, and competition opportunities. One of the pivotal moments in Hoy's career was his enrollment in the British Cycling Academy. The goal of the academy, which was run by people like Dave Brailsford and Peter Keen, was to develop elite cyclists who could compete at the greatest levels. Modern training methods, sports science, and nutrition programs were all introduced to Hoy, which aided in his quick development.

His emphasis on track cycling sprint events was one of the main facets of Hoy's development during this period. Rapid power and timing are essential for sprinting, and Hoy's experience racing BMX gave him an edge in these areas. He additionally profited from the experience of coaches such as Iain Dyer, who helped him hone his skills and cultivate the mental toughness necessary for success in demanding sprint competitions.

With a silver medal in the team sprint at the 1999 World Championships in Berlin, Hoy achieved his first significant senior success. He made his Olympic debut in the 2000 Sydney Games, winning a silver medal in the same event, which came after this accomplishment. The beginning of one of the most remarkable careers in cycling history was paved with these early triumphs. Hoy decided to devote himself entirely to a cycling career after experiencing success in the late 1990s. Following his graduation with a degree in sports science, he made the decision to devote himself entirely to training and competition. Cycling, especially in Britain, was not as popular or profitable as it would become later, so this choice was not without risk. But Hoy's love for the game and confidence in his abilities propelled him to make the risk.

At this point, British Cycling was starting to receive more money and assistance, partly because of the National Lottery's investment in professional sports. Better facilities, more professional coaching, and more international competition opportunities for British cyclists were made possible by this additional funding. This increased support was crucial to Hoy's development in the early years of his career and benefited other athletes as well. At the 2002 Commonwealth Games in Manchester, Hoy won a gold medal in the 1 km time trial, one of his first notable accomplishments. Hoy's first major international title made this victory a significant turning point in his career. Following his triumph at the Commonwealth Games, Hoy felt confident enough to compete at the sport's top level.

After his triumph at the Commonwealth Games, Hoy's early career reached its zenith at the 2004 Olympics in Athens. His numerous world titles in the 1 km time trial in previous years put him as the favorite going into the Games. Hoy thrived under the tremendous pressure. With a faultless performance in the 1 km time trial final, Hoy set a new Olympic record and took home the gold. Since it was his first Olympic gold and he became one of the world's top track cyclists, this triumph was a turning point in his career. At the UCI Track Cycling World Championships in 2004, Hoy won the gold medal in the 1 km time trial, which led to his first world championship. Hoy became one of the world's best sprinters after this triumph, which also paved the way for his subsequent supremacy in track cycling. Early in his career, Chris Hoy faced difficulties. He experienced injuries and competition disappointments, just like many other athletes. One of the biggest obstacles Hoy had to overcome was the Olympic Games' decision to remove the 1 km time trial event after 2004. In the discipline, Hoy was considered one of the best in the world and had won a silver medal at the 2000 Sydney Olympics. However, Hoy had to change his focus to other events like the sprint and the keirin since the event was removed from the Olympic schedule.

Hoy's career took a significant turn in 2004 with the Olympics in Athens. Setting an Olympic record, he won his first gold medal in the kilo session. In addition to making Hoy a formidable force in international cycling, this triumph stoked his dream of competing in the Olympics, which would propel him to even greater heights in the years to come. A major obstacle for Hoy after his triumph in Athens was the International Olympic Committee's (IOC) decision to drop the kilo from the Olympic program following the 2004 Games. Hoy took this as a chance to broaden his skill set and challenge himself, not a reason to give up. His versatility and will to stay at the top of his sport were evident as he concentrated on honing his skills in the sprint and keirin events.

Hoy's versatility paid off handsomely during the 2008 Beijing Olympics, where he won his biggest victory. He took home three gold medals in the individual, keirin, and team sprints in an incredible show of dominance. In a single Olympic Games, he became the first British athlete to win three gold medals in a century. He gained international recognition for his performance in Beijing, which solidified his place as a cycling legend. He was also named the BBC Sports Personality of the Year for 2008.

The victory in Beijing was a major turning point for British cycling in general as well as a personal victory for Hoy. In addition to encouraging a new generation of riders to take up cycling, his accomplishments and those of his teammates helped to increase cycling's visibility in the UK. A golden age of British cycling began during this time, with Hoy leading the charge in a wave of success that would last for many years. Hoy kept up his high-level competition after his victory in Beijing, adding to his remarkable medal haul at the World Championships and other international events. Even though he was 36 years old and nearing the end of his competitive career, he carried the same focus and determination into the 2012 London Olympics as he had throughout his career.

Hoy's Olympic career ended with a fitting conclusion at the 2012 Games. He secured two additional gold medals in the team sprint and keirin while competing domestically in front of enthusiastic spectators. These triumphs increased his total number of Olympic gold medals to six, making him the most successful British Olympian in history (a record that Jason Kenny later matched). Hoy's impact on the sport and his status as a national hero were demonstrated by the poignant moments as he celebrated his last Olympic victory in the keirin.

After retiring from competitive cycling following the 2012 Olympics, Hoy continued to be very active in the sport. He started selling his own line of bicycles that were made to accommodate riders of all skill levels. Through this business, he was able to spread his knowledge and love of cycling to a larger audience, making it more accessible to individuals from all walks of life.

Hoy's business endeavors are complemented by his involvement in a number of sport and cycling-related charitable causes. He has worked with organizations that use sport as a tool for education and social development, as well as those that advocate cycling as a way to enhance mental and physical health. It is well known that Hoy has made significant contributions to cycling and sports in general. A Member of the Order of the British Empire (MBE) for services to cycling, he was named in 2005. In the 2009 New Year's Honours list, he was knighted and became Sir Chris Hoy. These accolades are a testament to not only his athletic accomplishments but also his positive impact on British sport and his function as an ambassador for cycling.

Chapter 3
Chris Hoy's Development: Rise to Fame in Track Cycling

Hoy's first significant international success occurred during the Olympics in Sydney in 2000. After being chosen, he participated in the team sprint event for the British track cycling team. The silver medal was won by the British team, which featured riders like Craig MacLean and Jason Queally. This was Hoy's first Olympic victory.

Hoy made consistent strides in the international arena in the years preceding the 2000 Sydney Olympics. In the team sprint at his first World Championships in 1996, he placed tenth. He improved over the following few years and went on to win silver in the team sprint at the World Championships in 1999 and 2000. When Hoy made his Olympic debut in Sydney, he concentrated mostly on the sprint events. Three riders compete against the clock in the Olympic Sprint, also known as the team sprint, which is a track cycling event. While Queally led the first lap and MacLean anchored the last, Hoy's job on the team was to ride the second lap. The French team, who were the favorites and featured seasoned riders like Florian Rousseau and Laurent Gané, set the trio up for fierce competition. Even though they tried their hardest, the British team was unable to keep up with the French and finished in 44.349 seconds, missing out on the silver medal to France, who finished in 43.922 seconds.

The Olympics in Sydney were a watershed in Hoy's career. He was chosen at the age of 24 to compete in the team sprint event for Great Britain with Craig MacLean and Jason Queally. Prior to the Games, the three had been working out closely together to improve their strength and speed as well as their technique. Hoy took to the track with his teammates on September 16, 2000, at Sydney's Dunc Gray Velodrome. As the world's top track cyclists competed for Olympic glory, thousands of spectators crammed into the arena, creating an electrifying atmosphere. With their time of 44.680 seconds in the qualifying round, the British team guaranteed their spot in the medal rounds. Both the German and French teams, who were favored to win the gold medal, put up a fierce fight against them.

Great Britain and Germany played each other in the semifinals. The gold medal final against France was secured after Hoy and his teammates defeated their rivals in an exciting race. In a thrilling match, both teams gave it their all during the final. With a final time of 44.233 seconds, the French team consisting of Florian Rousseau, Arnaud Tournant, and Laurent Gané won the gold medal because they were simply too strong. After finishing with a time of 44.809 seconds, the British team secured the silver medal, only 0.576 seconds behind. Hoy's dream came true when he stood on the Olympic podium and accepted his silver medal. The result of years of effort and commitment, it was evidence of his skill and tenacity. Being one of just two cycling medals brought home by the nation from the Sydney Games, the medal also represented a major turning point for British cycling.

After winning the Olympics in Sydney, Hoy kept improving. In 2002, he represented Scotland at the Commonwealth Games held in Manchester. Because it gave him the opportunity to compete in front of his home crowd and represent his nation on a major international stage, Hoy saw the Commonwealth Games as a significant event. By this point, he had improved even more and was becoming one of the best track cyclists in the world. At the Manchester Games, Hoy had the opportunity to compete in front of his home crowd, as the velodrome was crowded with fervent British supporters. Hoy participated in the Manchester 1km time trial, which would later become one of his specialties. In cycling circles, the kilo is a demanding test of endurance and speed where competitors must finish four laps of the 250-meter track as fast as they can from a standing start.

With a silver medal in the 1 km time trial, Hoy put on a great show at the Games. The "kilo," as it is also called, would turn into one of Hoy's signature races, and his triumph in Manchester was a precursor to what was to come.

One of the most successful events in Hoy's early international career was the 1 km time trial, which was a race against the clock. Explosive power, endurance, and precise pacing are all necessary for the event, and Hoy's riding skills were all well-suited for them. In the UCI Track Cycling World Championships' 1 km time trial in 2002, Hoy took home his first world championship. His career reached a significant turning point with this triumph, which also made him one of the world's best track cyclists. In the kilo, Hoy was a fierce competitor who would dominate the sport for many years due to his ability to exert tremendous power over a comparatively short distance.

Hoy competed in the kilo final on the track on August 1, 2002. There was a lot of pressure because the home crowd was counting on their local hero to do great things. Hoy wasn't let down. With remarkable speed and accuracy, he went around the track and stopped the clock at 1:01.726. He set a new Commonwealth Games record in addition to winning the gold medal with this incredible time. Hoy's achievements in Manchester went beyond the kilogram. In the team sprint competition, he teamed up with fellow Scots Craig MacLean and Ross Edgar. The Australian team won the silver medal, but the three of them gave a great performance. Hoy became a hero in his home country of Scotland and one of the Games' biggest stars thanks to his two medals.

One of Hoy's career turning points was the 2002 Commonwealth Games. His performances in Manchester showed that he was a versatile rider, performing well in both solo and group competitions. It also demonstrated his capacity to function well under duress, a talent that would be useful to him in his professional life. After his Manchester triumph, Hoy turned his attention to the 2006 Commonwealth Games in Melbourne, Australia. In the four years in between the Games, Hoy had kept getting better, setting a new world record in the kilo and taking home several World Championship titles. Once more, Hoy lined up for the kilo final on March 17, 2006. Several elite riders competed for the gold medal in a fierce competition. Hoy put on an incredible ride, using all of his strength and experience. His time of 1:01.569 allowed him to set a new Games record and win his second consecutive Commonwealth gold medal.

Hoy found this victory especially sweet. It not only confirmed that he was the greatest kilo rider in the world, but it also offered some solace for the event's exclusion from the Olympic schedule. As evidence of the event's ongoing significance in track cycling, Hoy's supremacy in the kilo at the Commonwealth Games helped to maintain its public awareness. Nevertheless, Hoy wasn't satisfied with just one gold in Melbourne. He also participated in the team sprint, where he and Ross Edgar were partnered with Craig MacLean once more. With a time of 44.282 seconds, the Scottish trio narrowly defeated the English team before winning the gold medal. Hoy was further solidified as one of the best track cyclists of his generation by his double gold medal performance in Melbourne. Hoy's increasing accomplishments in world titles and the Olympics complemented his Commonwealth Games triumphs. His triumphs at the Olympics, especially in 2004 and 2008, where he won numerous gold medals, were made possible by his performances in the kilo and other sprint events. Nonetheless, his silver in 2006 and his first Commonwealth Games gold in 2002 continue to be significant turning points in his career, demonstrating his readiness to compete under pressure in important international tournaments and his dedication to representing Scotland internationally.

Chapter 4
Olympic Triumphs for Hoy: London (2012), Beijing (2008), and Athens (2004)

Sir Chris Hoy's career took a significant turn at the 2004 Olympic Games in Athens, establishing him as one of the most promising track cyclists in Great Britain. With a reputation as a top-tier competitor in the preceding years, Hoy came to Athens at the age of 28 with high hopes. The 1km time trial, which Hoy had been getting better at since his Olympic debut in Sydney 2000, was his main focus in Athens. Known as the "kilo," it was a demanding test of endurance, power, and speed that required riders to finish four laps of the velodrome as fast as they could from a standing start. At the Olympic Velodrome in Athens, Hoy took to the track on August 20, 2004. Given that he was a front-runner for the gold medal, the pressure was tremendous. Hoy had been very careful in his preparation, spending many hours with his British Cycling coaches improving his strength and technique.

With a remarkable time of 1 minute 0.711 seconds on the day of the competition, Hoy put on an outstanding performance. He set a new Olympic record in addition to winning the gold medal with this time. He faced fierce opposition, including his primary opponent, Frenchman Arnaud Tournant, who held the world record at the time, which made his victory remarkable. During Hoy's arrival at the starting gate, the velodrome became quiet. The kilo relied heavily on the explosive start, and Hoy's years of preparation paid off as he blasted out of the gate with immense strength. He set the tone for the remainder of his ride with a blisteringly fast first lap. Hoy persevered in his amazing pace, despite the burning sensation in his legs and lungs, lap after lap. The clock stopped at

1:00.711, a new Olympic record, as he crossed the finish line. The remaining riders tried to beat his mark, but Hoy still had to wait nervously even though the time was quicker than any other competitor had managed.

Eventually, Hoy's time held firm. His first Olympic victory in the kilo had come from winning the gold medal. This win was not only a major milestone for British cycling, but it was also a personal victory for Hoy. It marked a new era of dominance for the country in track cycling and was Great Britain's first gold medal since 1908. In Athens, Hoy's achievements went beyond just winning a gold medal for himself. Together with Jason Queally and Jamie Staff, he was a member of the British squad that won silver in the team sprint. This extra medal demonstrated Hoy's versatility and value to the British cycling team even more.

As a result of his success in Athens, Hoy gained widespread recognition in Britain. His friendly demeanor and evident love for his sport made him a well-liked public figure and media personality. Along with the gold medal came higher expectations for subsequent contests, which Hoy would both meet and surpass in the years to follow. For Sir Chris Hoy, the 2008 Olympic Games in Beijing presented a fresh obstacle. The elimination of the kilo from the Olympic program forced Hoy to shift his attention to other competitions. While a less talented athlete might have failed during this transitional phase, Hoy handled it with his usual tenacity and maturity. Hoy came to Beijing with the intention of building on Athens' success as a member of a formidable British cycling team. One of the greatest cycling performances in Olympic history would take place at the Beijing velodrome.

Team sprint was Hoy's first event in Beijing, where he competed with Jamie Staff and Jason Kenny. The trio from Britain had been playing well before the Games, and they performed admirably. The British team outperformed France in the gold medal final, setting a new world record time of 42.950 seconds and winning the gold. For Hoy, this triumph set the stage for an incredible Olympic campaign. Following the removal of the kilo, Hoy had been concentrating on the keirin. Keirins are a special and frequently erratic event that calls for both tactical skill and lightning-fast reflexes. Throughout the preliminary rounds, Hoy won each of his heats with ease and skill. The motorized bike known as the derny, which paces the riders for the first few laps, pulled off the track, giving Hoy a strong position in the final. Hoy's devastating burst of speed as the sprint for the line started allowed him to smash past his competitors and win his second gold medal of the Games. Because it showed that he could succeed at the highest level in a new discipline, this victory was especially sweet for Hoy.

Hoy, however, was not done yet. The individual sprint, a competition typically dominated by discipline experts, was his last event in Beijing. Prior to the competition, Hoy was not regarded as the favorite, despite his recent improvements in the sprint. Once more, Hoy's readiness and resolve were evident. He advanced through the stages, using a combination of strong physical prowess and strategic acumen to defeat elite opponents. In the gold medal final, Hoy competed against Jason Kenny, a younger teammate. Hoy won his third gold medal of the Games in a show of dominance, winning the best-of-three competition in straight rides. Hoy made history with this triumph, becoming the first British Olympian to win three gold medals at one Olympic Games in a century. With this accomplishment, he became a national hero and solidified his place in British sporting history. When Hoy performed in Beijing, it was truly amazing. Great Britain's dominance in cycling is evident from the fact that the country topped the medal table thanks in large part to his three gold medals. In addition to raising awareness of cycling as a sport, Hoy and his teammates' success served as motivation for a new generation of cyclists in the UK.

Hoy received a lot of praise following the Beijing Games. In 2008, he was recognized for his sporting accomplishments and popularity with the British public by being named BBC Sports Personality of the Year. For his services to sport, Prince Charles knighted him at Buckingham Palace in 2009, making him Sir Chris Hoy. The Beijing Olympics were the apex of Hoy's career to date, but they also raised the bar for his subsequent accomplishments. Hoy knew he would be under tremendous pressure to defend his titles at home during the 2012 London Olympics. With the London 2012 Olympic Games, Sir Chris Hoy had a once-in-a-lifetime opportunity to compete for Olympic gold in front of his home crowd. There was an additional level of significance to Hoy's performance because, at 36, he was aware that this would probably be his last Olympic appearance. A great deal of excitement surrounded Hoy's participation in the London Games. As one of Team GB's most accomplished Olympians, he bore the burden of the country's aspirations. The venue for Hoy's last Olympic campaign would be the recently constructed velodrome in London's Olympic Park, known as the "Pringle" because of its unusual shape.

Hoy once again teamed up with Jason Kenny and Philip Hindes for the team sprint, which was his first event in London. Though they faced fierce competition from countries like France and Germany, the trio had been playing very well before the Games. The lead-off rider, Philip Hindes, almost lost his footing shortly after the start of the qualifying round. The team did, however, get a restart, and they took full advantage of it. The British team had an incredible performance in the final against France, winning the gold medal and setting a new world record time of 42.600 seconds.

Hoy was especially emotional about this win. His fifth Olympic gold medal tied Sir Steve Redgrave's record for the most British athletes. As Hoy crossed the finish line, the home crowd's thunderous cheers were a testament to the encouragement and respect he received. Now that he had won the team sprint gold, Hoy turned his attention to the keirin, the event he had won in Beijing. There was a lot of pressure on Hoy to maintain his title and possibly beat Redgrave's record.

Hoy advanced through the early stages using his signature blend of raw strength and tactical acumen. He was positioned well when the derny pulled off the track in the final. Hoy's devastating turn of speed as the sprint for the line started allowed him to smash past his competitors and win his second Olympic gold medal overall. Hoy was widely praised in the years following the London Olympics. Numerous people in the UK praised his accomplishments and hailed him as one of the greatest British athletes of all time. His and his teammates' achievements contributed significantly to the rising popularity of cycling as a recreational and competitive sport throughout the nation. The 2012 cycling events' focal point, the London Velodrome, was later renamed the Lee Valley VeloPark in Hoy's honor, further cementing his legacy in British sport.

After winning in London, Hoy's Olympic career ended. Six gold medals and one silver medal were his total from four Olympic Games.

Chapter 5
The World Championship Accomplishments and Retirement of Professional Cyclist Sir Chris Hoy

In his career, Sir Chris Hoy became one of the most illustrious and successful track cyclists in history, winning an astounding 11 World Championships in a variety of events. His legacy as a cycling legend was firmly established by his performances at the UCI Track Cycling World Championships. Hoy won his first gold medal at the World Championship in the team sprint event in 2002. Alongside fellow British riders Jamie Staff and Jason Queally, Hoy contributed to the British team's triumph in Copenhagen, Denmark. The start of Hoy's more than ten-year run of success at the World Championships was this.

Hoy's first individual World Championship victory came in the 1km time trial in Melbourne, Australia, in 2004. In the early years of his career, Hoy had focused on the "kilo" event, and his triumph confirmed his place as the best in the world. Hoy's fantastic power output over the distance was demonstrated by his winning time of 1:00.711, which was just short of the world record. Hoy put on another strong showing at the 2005 World Championships in Los Angeles, successfully defending his 1km time trial title. Gold was won by him ahead of Dutch rider Theo Bos at 1:00.999. This consecutive triumph enhanced Hoy's standing as the kilo event's man to beat.

Hoy had to change his focus to other events, though, when the 1km time trial was eliminatcd from the Olympic program after 2004. In order to reap the benefits in the upcoming years, he started focusing more on the shorter sprint events. Gold in the keirin at the 2006

World Championships in Bordeaux, France, demonstrated Hoy's versatility. His first World Championship victory in a sprint event other than the kilo came from this victory. As Hoy made his way through the keirin heats and proceeded to win the final, his tactical skill and lightning-fast speed were clearly evident.

During the 2007 World Championships in Palma de Mallorca, Spain, Hoy achieved unprecedented success by winning three gold medals. For the second year in a row, he won the keirin. He also won the team sprint with Ross Edgar and Jamie Staff. Hoy's triumph in the individual sprint, however, was what really made his ascent to the title of all-around sprint champion. In the world's most prestigious sprint cycling event, Hoy defeated the current Olympic champion Ryan Bayley in the final, demonstrating his ability to compete with the best. Hoy's supremacy persisted in Manchester, England, during the 2008 World Championships. At home, Hoy delighted British spectators by successfully defending his sprint and keirin titles. In the gold medal final, he easily defeated longtime rival Theo Bos, making his sprint victory all the more impressive. At these World Championships, Hoy won three sprint events (keirin, sprint, and team sprint), which prepared him for his historic Olympic performance in Beijing later that year.

Hoy paused his competitive career after winning three gold medals at the 2008 Olympics and did not compete in the 2009 World Championships. But in 2010, he made a comeback to the international scene by participating in the World Championships in Copenhagen, Denmark. Despite not taking home any individual honors, Hoy, Jason Kenny, and Matt Crampton helped the British sprint team reclaim their world title. In an individual event, Hoy returned to the top of the podium at the 2011 World Championships in Apeldoorn, Netherlands. He defeated rival Gregory Bauge in an exciting keirin final, stifling a fierce challenge with his signature power. With this triumph, Hoy's total number of gold medals at the World Championship reached 10. Before the London Olympics in 2012, Hoy participated in his last World Championships. Hoy would have one final opportunity to improve his form prior to his home Olympics at these championships, which would be held in Melbourne, Australia. Not to be outdone, Hoy won gold in the keirin, increasing his total number of World Championship victories to 11. An appropriate conclusion to Hoy's remarkable run of success at the world championships was this last world title.

Hoy's triumph at the World Championships was also a major factor in the rise of Great Britain as a dominant force in track cycling. Along with the triumphs of teammates Bradley Wiggins and Victoria Pendleton, he helped British Cycling develop a winning culture that would lead to an unprecedented level of success at the Olympic Games. At the age of 37, Sir Chris Hoy announced his retirement from professional cycling on April 18, 2013. The decision was made less than a year after he made history at the 2012 London Olympics, where he won two gold medals and became the most successful Olympian in Great Britain's history with six gold medals. Hoy was getting close to the age of 37, when it was getting harder to continue performing at his best. Hoy admitted that he was unable to generate the same power outputs that had allowed him to remain so dominant in earlier years when he announced his retirement. He said, "I've always said that I would step away from the sport at the top and not go on too long. I don't want to turn up to the Commonwealth Games as a shadow of my former self." The Commonwealth Games was mentioned, which was important because the 2014

Games were scheduled to take place in Glasgow, Scotland, where Hoy is from. A lot of people wanted to see Hoy compete one final time in his native country, but he knew he couldn't perform to the standard he expected.

Hoy also made the decision because he wanted to end the sport on a positive note. His competitive career ended well with his performance at the London Olympics, where he took home gold in the keirin and team sprint. Hoy considered winning Olympic gold in front of his home crowd at the London Velodrome—later renamed in his honor—to be the ultimate way to cap off his career as a professional athlete.

At the same time that Hoy retired, British Cycling was going through a generational change. Younger riders, such as Jason Kenny, were prepared to assume leadership positions after proving themselves to be a deserving Hoy successor in the sprint events. Having acknowledged the significance of creating space for the upcoming generation of talent, Hoy said, "I'm happy with this decision and I'm looking forward to the next chapter in my life." Retirement also gave Hoy the opportunity to pursue new challenges and interests. After taking up motor racing, he participated in a number of races, including the 2016 24 Hours of Le Mans. The successful transition between cycling events during Hoy's career was akin to this new endeavor, which demonstrated his competitive spirit and versatility. Perhaps the greatest example of Hoy's influence on British sport is the accolades he has accumulated since retiring. His outstanding contributions to cycling and British sport in general were recognized in 2013 when he received the BBC Sports Personality of the Year Lifetime Achievement Award. The London Velodrome has been renamed the Lee Valley VeloPark Chris Hoy Velodrome in order to preserve his legacy and encourage cyclists for years to come.

Sir Chris Hoy's career total at the UCI Track Cycling World Championships was 11 gold, 6 silver, and 1 bronze. One of the most successful track cyclists in history, he excelled in a variety of disciplines, including the kilo, sprint, keirin, and team sprint.

Since his retirement, Hoy has become an author as well, writing a number of books, including an autobiography and a series of children's books that encourage young people to start riding bicycles. Hoy's literary pursuits have given him the opportunity to spread his love of the game and remain an inspiration to future athletes. Additionally, retirement gave Hoy more time to devote to his family. The couple's first child, Callum, was born in 2014, and their second child, Chloe, was born in 2017. Because of his son's early birth and subsequent prolonged stay in the neonatal unit, Hoy has been candid about the pleasures and difficulties of fatherhood. As a result of this encounter, Hoy became a fervent advocate for charities that support premature birth, leveraging his position to increase awareness and financial support for this crucial cause.

Chapter 6
After-Cycling Career and Chris Hoy's Non-Sport Life

By following his passion for motorsport, Sir Chris Hoy started an exciting new chapter in his sporting career after retiring from professional cycling in 2013. He developed a lifelong passion for cars and racing from an early age, which propelled him to switch from two wheels to four wheels. The British GT Championship was Hoy's first foray into competitive motorsport in 2014. He represented the Nissan team in the GT4 class, piloting a Nissan GT-R NISMO GT3. Nissan's Driver Development Program, which aimed to transform athletes from other sports into successful racing drivers, included this move. Hoy displayed a great deal of promise and versatility in his first season. In collaboration with seasoned driver Wolfgang Reip, he produced a number of noteworthy outcomes. They achieved a podium finish at Spa-Francorchamps, in Belgium, which was one of their most impressive performances.

Building on his encouraging beginning, Hoy furthered his skill development and experience in a number of racing series. He participated in the 2015 European Le Mans Series (ELMS) as a member of the LMP3 class. This transition to prototype racing was difficult because these cars demand a different skill set than GT racing.

Hoy made quick progress, demonstrating his dedication to his new sport. He was a member of Team LNT

Ginetta-Nissan with Charlie Robertson, and the two of them were incredibly successful. In addition to winning the season's first round at Silverstone, they also triumphed at Red Bull Ring in Austria. The LMP3 class championship was won by Hoy and Robertson in their rookie year as a result of these victories as well as their steady performances throughout the season. The highlight of Hoy's motorsport career was competing in the renowned 24 Hours of Le Mans in 2016, fulfilling a lifelong dream. This legendary endurance race, which joins the Indianapolis 500 and the Monaco Grand Prix as part of the Triple Crown of Motorsport, is regarded as one of the most difficult and prominent motorsport competitions.

Hoy drove a Ligier JS P2-Nissan algarve pro racing in the LMP2 class. He was with Michael Munemann and Andrea Pizzitola in the car. In this demanding test of man and machine, Hoy performed admirably, even though he was relatively new to endurance racing. The team finished 32nd overall out of 60 starters and 17th in their class after completing 341 laps. Due to the high attrition rate and the intense physical and mental strain of competing for twenty-four hours straight, Hoy considered simply finishing the race to be a feat.

Using his reputation, experience, and love of cycling, Sir Chris Hoy has launched a number of profitable business endeavors since retiring from professional cycling. These businesses have given him the opportunity to pursue new business challenges while maintaining a connection to the cycling community. Hoy has launched his own bicycle brand, HOY Bikes, which has been one of his most important business endeavors. With the goal of creating top-notch bicycles for both adults and kids, HOY Bikes was founded in 2013 in collaboration with Evans Cycles, a significant UK cycling retailer. The brand's philosophy mirrors Hoy's own riding style, emphasizing the development of bikes that are affordable, pleasurable, and highly functional.

A variety of children's bikes were initially part of the HOY Bikes line, along with adult road bikes and hybrid bikes. Hoy had a special place in his heart for the kids' line because he wanted to make bikes that would encourage young people to take up cycling. In order to make these bikes comfortable and manageable, the proportions and riding preferences of children were carefully taken into account. Apart from HOY Bikes, Sir Chris has also dabbled in the realm of cycling clothing and accessories. Several brands have partnered with him to produce goods that are named after him and showcase his skills. He collaborated, for instance, with Sky HD to develop a line of sunglasses intended especially for cyclists. Hoy himself provided input when creating these sunglasses, adding features that he felt were crucial to his racing career. Additionally, Hoy has branded and consulted on a variety of cycling apparel. He introduced the HOY Vulpine clothing line in 2014 in association with the British cycling apparel brand Vulpine. This collection featured both casual apparel with a cycling theme and performance cycling apparel. The collection reflected Hoy's belief that cycling should be accessible to everyone and was made to appeal to both serious cyclists and those who just enjoy the cycling lifestyle.

For Hoy, the fitness technology industry has been another important business endeavor. A prominent producer of indoor training bikes, Wattbike, teamed up with Hoy after realizing the growing popularity of indoor cycling and virtual training platforms. Through his experience, he has contributed to the creation of indoor training environments that closely resemble cycling in the real world, helping to develop and market Wattbike products. The relationship between Hoy and Wattbike goes beyond merely endorsing the brand. Using his background as an elite athlete, he has been actively active in developing training plans and content for Wattbike users, assisting riders of all skill levels in enhancing their performance. Hoy is able to stay on the cutting edge of advancements in indoor training thanks to this endeavor, which combines his love of cycling with the newest fitness technology. Hoy has pursued business endeavors beyond just cycling-related goods. Opportunities in other fields, such as children's books, have also been investigated by him. He co-wrote a series of children's books called "Flying Fergus," which was published in 2020. A young boy's adventures with his magical bicycle are the focus of these books, which hope to encourage kids to love riding and follow their aspirations. With its blend of thrilling tales and inspirational quotes about tenacity, camaraderie, and the love of riding a bike, the series has been well received.

The transition of Sir Chris Hoy from professional athlete to media personality has been seamless and complex. He has maintained his public profile and continued to have an impact on the sport world long after he retired from competitive cycling thanks to his charisma, eloquent personality, and extensive cycling knowledge, which have made him a sought-after figure in a variety of media attempts. As a commentator and analyst for major cycling events, Hoy has held some of the most prominent media positions. In particular, his knowledge and perception have been invaluable when covering the Olympic Games. Hoy was an integral member of the BBC's cycling commentary team during the 2016 Rio Olympics and the 2020 Tokyo Olympics (which were postponed until 2021 due to the COVID-19 pandemic). His capacity to deconstruct intricate racing tactics and offer firsthand insight into the experiences of athletes has been highly commended, enhancing the coverage's nuance and realism.

Hoy has frequently presided over the Tour de France, the World Championships, and other track cycling competitions in addition to the Olympics. He increases the number of people who watch cycling events by combining technical knowledge with the ability to make the sport understandable to non-sports fans. Apart from live commentary, Hoy has appeared in a lot of feature shows and documentaries about cycling. He has given talks and appeared on programs that examine cycling's history, the science underlying the sport, and the individual tales of athletes. These programs have given Hoy the opportunity to demonstrate his expertise and love of cycling in a more thorough manner, frequently highlighting facets of the sport that casual enthusiasts might not be familiar with.

Additionally, Hoy has dabbled in writing books. His non-fiction books include the children's book series "Flying Fergus," among others. "Chris Hoy: The Autobiography," his 2009 autobiography, offers a detailed account of his path to Olympic glory. He then published "How to Ride a Bike: From Starting Out to Peak Performance" in 2018, a thorough manual that blends career insights with useful cycling tips. Hoy has made a name for himself in the market for motivational speaking. Speaking at conferences for sports, schools, and corporations, he regularly shares insights from his athletic career that can be used to advance both personally and professionally. Through these speaking engagements, he has been able to encourage and uplift individuals in a variety of fields, greatly expanding his influence outside of the realm of sports.

Following his cycling career, Sir Chris Hoy has been heavily involved in philanthropy. He has supported causes that are important to him by participating in a variety of charitable endeavors. His longstanding dedication includes his role as an ambassador for the nonprofit organization Children's Hospices Across Scotland (CHAS). Hoy is involved with CHAS, which cares for children with life-threatening illnesses. In addition to raising money, Hoy spends time with the families and kids the charity helps. The issues faced by families dealing with life-threatening illnesses have become more visible thanks to his contributions, which have also helped to raise awareness of the work that CHAS does. A charity that offers financial support to young British athletes, SportsAid, has also received Hoy's unwavering support. The organization helped him in his early career, and he has since become an advocate and mentor, helping to support the upcoming generation of athletes. Participating in fundraising events and advising young athletes on how to handle the difficulties of pursuing careers in elite sports are two examples of his involvement.

Apart from these causes, Hoy has contributed to numerous other charitable endeavors. He has supported The Dallaglio Foundation, an initiative started by former England rugby captain Lawrence Dallaglio that aims to better the lives of youth by utilizing sport and education. A substantial amount of money has been raised to support programs that assist vulnerable youth thanks to

Hoy's involvement in foundation events, such as cycling challenges. Hoy has also contributed to fundraising campaigns for mental health awareness and cancer research. Hoy joined other athletes and celebrities in 2020 during the COVID-19 pandemic to support the National Health Service (NHS) and raise money for frontline workers through a variety of charitable endeavors.

Given his extensive involvement in charitable endeavors, Sir Chris Hoy's dedication to giving back to society and using his position for good is clear. His work supports a variety of causes, from community development and medical research to cycling and youth sports. Being an ambassador for UNICEF UK since 2009, this organization is one of Hoy's most important charitable affiliations. Through his work with UNICEF, he has traveled to many different countries and seen firsthand the struggles that children in developing nations face. In order to observe how UNICEF-provided bicycles were assisting children in obtaining healthcare and education, Hoy visited Malawi in 2014. His dedication to the organization's mission was reinforced by this profoundly impactful experience.

In the course of his work with UNICEF, Hoy has participated in a lot of fundraising events. Among the most noteworthy was his involvement in the 2014 Commonwealth Games appeal in Glasgow, which raised more than £5 million for children's initiatives throughout the Commonwealth and Scotland. Hoy's participation encouraged public participation and helped to increase the appeal's visibility. In the world of charities that focus on cycling, Hoy has long supported the Bike Hub program run by the Bicycle Association. By encouraging young people to ride and offering financial support for different cycling projects, this initiative seeks to protect cycling's future. Hoy's support and involvement have been essential in increasing awareness and funding for this cause.

Additionally, Hoy supports young cyclists who want to succeed in the sport by being a patron of the Braveheart Cycling Fund, a charity in Scotland. Promising young riders can access the equipment, training, and competition opportunities they require to hone their skills with the help of the fund. In addition to aiding in fund-raising, Hoy's participation serves as motivation for the young athletes the charity supports. Hoy has a special place in his heart for Cycling Projects, a charity that organizes the Wheels for All campaign. This program uses a network of inclusive cycling centers throughout the UK to make cycling accessible to people of all abilities. Hoy has been a vocal supporter of this cause, stressing the value of enabling bike riding for all people, irrespective of their physical or mental limitations.

Sarra Kemp, who practices law, is Sir Chris Hoy's spouse. 43-year-old Sarra may not be as well-known as her husband, but she has built a prosperous career for herself. At Edinburgh-based Balfour and Manson, she practices personal injury law as a solicitor. A mutual friend threw a party at Edinburgh's Grand Cru bar in 2008, where the couple first met. Sarra accompanied Hoy during his spectacular Olympic triple crown triumph in Beijing. Hoy proposed to her with a diamond ring during a romantic trip to Prague in 2009, and she gladly accepted.

For their wedding, Sarra wore a white wedding gown with a veil, and Hoy wore a grey kilt, sporran, and grey jacket. The location was only disclosed to guests at the very last minute, and the ceremony was kept a secret. Sadly, flight restrictions brought on by volcanic ash prevented many invitees from attending. Following their marriage ceremony at Edinburgh's St. Giles' Cathedral, the couple hosted a reception at the famed Signet Library. Sarra, looking stunning in an ivory gown with a flowing train and veil, waved to the assembled crowd on the Royal Mile in Edinburgh before entering the cathedral. Upon her arrival, a street piper began playing "The Highland Wedding," drawing additional curious bystanders.

Despite efforts to keep the ceremony private, attention was drawn by the presence of a TV crew, photographers, and vintage Jaguars. When word got out, tourists joined the crowd. As a matter of fact, the wedding was so secret that guests were only told the venue on the day of the event. They were told to meet in the heart of Edinburgh and that the ceremony would take place at St Giles, also called the High Kirk of Edinburgh.

There were many guests to celebrate, including men dressed in Highland garb. Rebecca Adlington, the Olympic gold medallist swimmer, was one of them. When Hoy's 18-month-old godson, Hector Robinson, became restless, his father, Alasdair, had to take him outside, so he missed a lot of the ceremony. When St. Giles' doors opened following the ceremony, the newlyweds came out beaming with happiness. The audience cheered as Hoy, wearing a charcoal jacket and a grey tartan kilt, stood next to his bride. His ushers and bridesmaids were dressed in black with charcoal accents and kilts that matched.

For the special day, the couple was joined by university friends from St Andrews and Moray House as well as old school friends from George Watson's College. The photographers pushed Hoy to kiss Sarra as they posed for pictures, but he smiled and waved to the audience before they headed to the Signet Library for the reception. While continuing to practice law, Sarra, now known as Sarra Hoy, assumed a more prominent role as the spouse of one of the most well-known athletes in Britain. It was revealed in 2014 that Chris and Sarra Hoy were expecting their first child. Their path to parenthood, however, took a surprising turn on October 15, 2014, when their son, Callum David Robert Hoy, was born 11 weeks early. Callum needed special care in the neonatal unit because he was only 2 pounds 2 ounces at birth. A new member of the Hoy family was welcomed in 2019. September 9, 2019, saw the birth of Chloe Rose Hoy, who joined her older brother Callum. Because Chloe's birth was uneventful, the family was able to enjoy a more normal newborn phase, unlike her brother's dramatic early arrival.

Significant difficulties have been faced by the Hoy family since the year began. After more than a year of learning about his terminal cancer diagnosis, Chris Hoy made the news public in February 2024. On the other hand, Hoy said he still feels "fortunate."

When he first went to the doctor in September 2023 because of shoulder pain, his cancer was discovered. Subsequent scans revealed that the primary cancer was in his prostate, and a tumor was discovered there. His ribs, spine, pelvis, and shoulder were among the areas of his body where the disease had spread. Despite his diagnosis, Sir Hoy, who was knighted in 2008 while still participating in sports, is still active. He recently took part in PACE October's wellness week event in Greece, where he completed seven bike rides in five days. He was diagnosed with terminal multiple sclerosis (MS), and his wife of 14 years, Sarra, is coping with "very active and aggressive" MS. She was diagnosed with multiple sclerosis (MS), a degenerative disease that has no known cure, after her doctor recommended a scan after she started to experience tingling in her face and tongue. Sarra's husband was already struggling with his prognosis of only "two to four years" to live, so she decided to wait until December to tell him of her diagnosis until November 2023. Despite everything, Hoy is still involved, as evidenced by his recent attendance at PACE October.

Printed in Great Britain
by Amazon